**NORTH
LINCOLNSHIRE**
COUNCIL

Library items can be renewed online 24/7, you
will need your library card number and PIN.

Avoid library overdue charges by signing up to
receive email preoverdue reminders at

http://www.opac.northlincs.gov.uk/

Follow us on Facebook
www.facebook.com/northlincolnshirelibraries

www.northlincs.gov.uk/libraries

SPACE

BY
JOANNA BRUNDLE

SCIENCE IN ACTION

©2018
Book Life
King's Lynn
Norfolk PE30 4LS

ISBN: 978-1-78637-226-0

A catalogue record for this book
is available from the British Library.

Written by:
Joanna Brundle

Edited by:
Kirsty Holmes

Designed by:
Drue Rintoul

Photocredits
Abbreviations: l-left, r-right, b-bottom, t-top, c-centre, m-middle.

Front Cover t – cigdem. Front Cover mt, mb – Vadim Sadovski. Front Cover b – solarseven. 1,2 – Vadim Sadovski. 4t – Markus Gann. 4b – PlanilAstro. 5t – Castlesk. 5bl – Andrew Roland. 5br – iryna. 6br – By Maximilien Brice, CERN (CERN Document Server) [CC BY-SA 3.0 (http://creativecommons.org/licenses/by-sa/3.0)], via Wikimedia Commons. 7t – angelinast. 7ml – MarcelClemens. 7bl – Bill Frische. 8t – BlueRingMedia. 8b – Krissanapong Wongsawarng. 9t – Aphelleon. 9tr – Taras Vyshnya. 9b – fluidworkshop. 10 & 11 bg – guteksk7. 10t – Vadim Sadovski. 10m – NASA images. 10b – Vadim Sadovski. 11 – Vadim Sadovski. 12b – AZSTARMAN. 13t – Igor Chekalin. 13m – Alex Mit. 13b – NASA images. 14l – Ad_hominem. 14bm – NASA images. 14br – Bill Frische. 15 – NASA images. 16t – Jurik Peter. 16b – NASA images. 17tr – Jurik Peter. 17tl – yurchak. 17br – KdEdesign. 18t – plotplot. 18mr – Bjoern Wylezich. 18b – Mario Savoia. 19m – MarcelClemens. 19b – By ESA/ATG medialab [CC BY-SA 2.0 (http://creativecommons.org/licenses/by-sa/2.0)], via Wikimedia Commons. 20l – Lukasz Janyst. 20tr – Nicku. 20b – Castleski. 21 – 3Dsculptor. 22b – Vadim Sadovski. 23t – sripfoto. 23b – Kongsak. 24 & 25b – PlanilAstro. 26tr – Nice to meet you. 26b – Paulo Afonso. 27t – Jurik Peter. 27br – Egyptian Studio. 27bl – Everett Historical. 28tr – Igor Zh. 28b – pathdoc. 29b – Bill Frische. 30tr – Nerthuz. 30b – Juergen Faelchle. Images are courtesy of Shutterstock.com. With thanks to Getty Images, Thinkstock Photo and iStockphoto.

CONTENTS

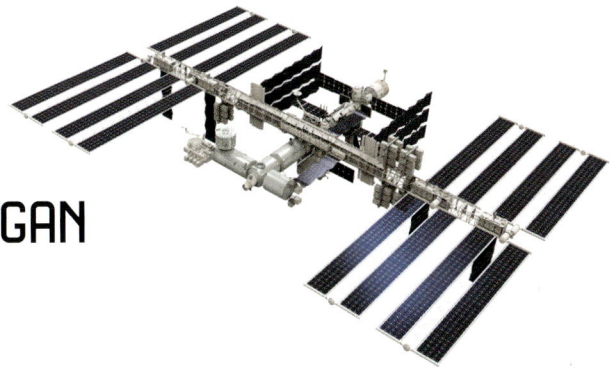

Words that look like **this** are explained in the glossary on page 31.

WHAT IS SPACE?

When it gets dark tonight, take a moment to look into the night sky. You'll be gazing into space. The universe is made up of planets, stars, **moons**, and other **matter** such as dust and gases... and space! Space is unbelievably enormous and scientists who study it, called astronomers, believe it is getting bigger all the time.

HOW BIG IS THE UNIVERSE?

The average distance between the Earth and the Sun is around 150 **million** kilometres. This is called an Astronomical Unit (AU). But this unit of measurement can't even begin to measure the distances between things in the wider universe, so light years are used instead.

Light travels faster than anything else in the universe at a speed of around 300,000 kilometres per second. A light year is the distance light travels in a year – 9,460,528,404,847 kilometres. Apart from the Sun, the closest star to Earth is Proxima Centauri, which is 4.24 light years away!

A trip to the Sun would be the same distance as travelling around the Earth, almost 4,000 times!

MOST SCIENTISTS BELIEVE THE UNIVERSE BEGAN AROUND 13.8 BILLION YEARS AGO.

Stars gather together in groups called galaxies. There are at least 100 **billion** galaxies in space, separated by millions of light years. The vastness of space is mind-boggling!

Our galaxy is called the Milky Way. The nearest galaxy to us is the Andromeda Galaxy. It is 2.5 million light years away!

Space is dark and silent. We are able to hear sound on Earth because **particles** in the air vibrate, sending the sound in waves to our ears. In space, there are almost no particles to vibrate and so space is very quiet.

It's very cold in space too. **Radiation** from our Sun heats the Earth's upper **atmosphere** to 120°C, but in outer space the average temperature is -270°C. Brrrrr!

EARLY DISCOVERIES

Sunrise Over Stonehenge

People have been fascinated with space since ancient times. Early Egyptian and Chinese civilisations made calendars by studying the movements of the planets. Before **satellites** were invented, sailors used maps charting the stars to work out where they were and to find their way.

Galileo Galilei
(1564-1642)

The prehistoric monument, Stonehenge, in the UK is believed to have connections with ancient astronomy. The stones are lined up with the sunrise on midsummer's day and with the sunset on midwinter's day.

An Italian astronomer, Galileo, was one of the first astronomers to study space using a **telescope**. He made many important discoveries, including the four largest moons that **orbit** the planet Jupiter. They are called the Galilean moons.

Early astronomers had no idea of the vastness of space. An Ancient Greek called Ptolemy (90-170 AD) believed the Earth was at the centre of the universe. To pronounce his name, say toll-a-mee.

HOW THE UNIVERSE BEGAN

Most scientists believe that the universe began as a tiny, very hot and dense speck of matter that exploded. The explosion is known as the Big Bang. The energy released from the explosion caused the universe to expand even faster than the speed of light.

GEORGES LEMAÎTRE

Georges Lemaître (1894-1966) was a Belgian scientist whose ideas led to the Big Bang **theory**. He thought that, since the universe was growing, it must have been smaller in the past. At some stage, it must have been a single point, which then exploded.

YOU CAN DEMONSTRATE HOW THE UNIVERSE IS EXPANDING BY DRAWING SOME PLANETS AND STARS ON A BALLOON. MEASURE THE DISTANCE BETWEEN THEM. NOW BLOW UP THE BALLOON AND RE-MEASURE. WHAT DO YOU NOTICE?

THE LARGE HADRON COLLIDER

Nobody was around to experience the Big Bang! So, scientists have tried to work out what happened, using experiments and mathematical models. The Large Hadron Collider, or LHC, completed in 2008, helps scientists with this work. It sits in a 27-kilometre tunnel, near Geneva in Switzerland. Particles are sent down the tunnel at almost the speed of light and are crashed into one another. This recreates what was happening minutes after the Big Bang, when particles with lots of energy would collide.

OVER 10,000 SCIENTISTS AND ENGINEERS FROM OVER 100 COUNTRIES WERE INVOLVED IN BUILDING THE LHC.

The Large Hadron Collider

AFTER THE BIG BANG

After only a few seconds, the particles that **atoms** are made of began to form. These particles are called neutrons, protons and electrons. The first atoms formed around 380,000 years later. The temperature had now cooled from around one billion to about 3,000°C. The first light, now known as cosmic background radiation, also appeared.

The first stars appeared around 400 million years after the Big Bang.

Over billions of years, the force of **gravity** pulled stars and other matter together, to form galaxies. More than nine billion years after the Big Bang, our Sun formed from a massive dust and gas cloud. The remains of this giant cloud eventually formed the planets, moons and other **celestial bodies** in the **solar system**.

SCIENTISTS CAN STILL DETECT THIS COSMIC BACKGROUND RADIATION. IT IS THE OLDEST FORM OF ENERGY AND GIVES SCIENTISTS LOTS OF CLUES ABOUT WHAT HAPPENED STRAIGHT AFTER THE BIG BANG.

This is Sirius – the brightest star in the night sky

There are between 200-400 million stars of different ages in the Milky Way galaxy alone.

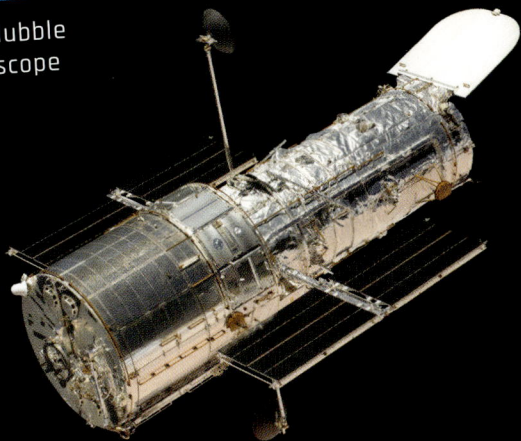
The Hubble Telescope

The Horsehead Nebula (Gas and Dust Cloud)

THE HUBBLE TELESCOPE

In the 1920s, an American astronomer called Edwin Hubble proved that the universe was not a fixed size. In fact, it was growing – or expanding. Hubble died in 1953 but, in April 1990, a telescope named after him was launched into space, aboard a **space shuttle** called Discovery. The telescope has beamed over a million pictures of space back to Earth.

It was once thought that galaxies didn't form until at least a billion years after the Big Bang. In March 2016, however, the oldest and most distant known galaxy was discovered, thanks to the Hubble Telescope. It formed just 400 million years after the Big Bang.

The Hubble Telescope orbits the Earth once every 97 minutes, sending back images of deep space, like this.

THE
SOLAR SYSTEM

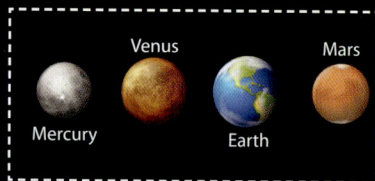

*Our solar system is made up of the Sun, eight planets, over 180 moons, smaller planets called dwarf planets, millions of **asteroids** and billions of **comets**. The Sun is at the centre of the solar system and the planets orbit around it. They are held in orbit by the pulling force of the Sun's gravity. As the solar system formed, small rocky planets appeared close to the Sun. Further away, temperatures were much lower. Here, large planets appeared, made mostly of the gases **hydrogen** and **helium**. They are known as gas giants.*

The Solar System

Mercury
Venus
Earth
Mars

Rocky Planets

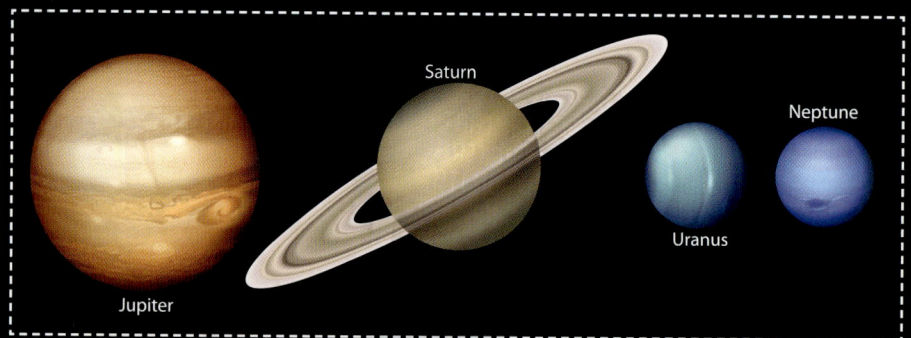

Jupiter
Saturn
Uranus
Neptune

Gas Giant Planets

THE SUN

The Sun is a star. From the Earth, it looks bigger and brighter than any other stars because it is by far the closest to us. It is a huge ball of gases, with a surface temperature of around 5,600°C. Sometimes cooler dark spots, called sunspots, can be detected. The Sun sometimes releases huge clouds of gases and particles in explosions called flares.

The Sun's flares produce spectacular displays of light called auroras, near the North and South Poles.

NEVER LOOK DIRECTLY AT THE SUN. IT CAN CAUSE SERIOUS, PERMANENT DAMAGE TO YOUR EYES, EVEN BLINDNESS.

THE EARTH

The Earth takes 365 days to complete its orbit around the Sun – or one year. We have seasons during the year because the Earth is tilted on its **axis** throughout its orbit, towards a star called Polaris or the Pole Star. The top and bottom halves of the Earth – the Northern and Southern Hemispheres – are tilted away from the Sun's warmth at opposite points in the orbit. That's why, for example, when it's summer in Europe, it's winter in Australia.

When people in Sydney, Australia are celebrating New Year at midnight, it is still only the afternoon of 31st of December in London, UK.

THE EARTH IS THE ONLY BODY IN THE SOLAR SYSTEM THAT HAS LIQUID WATER PERMANENTLY ON ITS SURFACE. THIS MAKES IT THE ONLY PLANET KNOWN TO SUPPORT LIFE.

THE MOON

The pull of the Earth's gravity keeps the Moon orbiting around the Earth. Each orbit takes around 27 days. It also takes about 27 days for the Moon to spin round or rotate once on its own axis.

Phases of the Moon

THE MOON DOESN'T GIVE OFF LIGHT – THERE IS NO SUCH THING AS MOONLIGHT! THE MOON SEEMS TO SHINE BECAUSE IT REFLECTS LIGHT FROM THE SUN.

Now that we've looked at our own planet, let's go on a space mission to investigate the other seven.

MERCURY

It's very hot on Mercury because it is so close to the Sun. The daytime temperature reaches 450°C! Mercury completes its orbit around the Sun in just 88 days. If you could live on Mercury, you would have four birthdays for every Earth year!

VENUS

Thick, yellowish clouds hide the surface of Venus. Its atmosphere is mostly made up of **carbon dioxide**, which acts like a giant heat blanket. Venus is the hottest planet, reaching 465°C on its surface.

MARS

Mars is half the Earth's size and is much colder – the temperature can fall to minus 140°C. Mars is often called the Red Planet because the ground is covered in brownish-rediron oxide (rust). The largest volcano in the solar system, Olympus Mons, is found on Mars.

JUPITER

Jupiter is over twice as big as all the other planets put together. It has 67 moons, the largest of which are Io, Europa, Callisto and Ganymede. Jupiter spins really fast – each day lasts less than ten hours. This fast spin whips up fierce storms. The Great Red Spot is a huge storm that has been raging for over 300 years.

The Great Red Spot

SATURN

Saturn is surrounded by spectacular rings, formed from billions of ice crystals and rocky **debris**. Saturn has powerful storms, with lightning bolts 10,000 times stronger than on Earth and wind speeds of up to 1,800 kilometres per hour. Saturn has over 60 moons. The largest moon, Titan, has rain and lakes made up of liquid **methane**.

URANUS

Uranus is unusual because it rolls along on its side, rather than spinning around an upright axis, like the other planets. Astronomers think it was tipped over billions of years ago by a collision with a huge planet-like object. All of Uranus' 27 moons are named after characters in the plays of the English playwright, William Shakespeare. One of the moons, Miranda, has canyons many times deeper than the Grand Canyon in the USA. Uranus also experiences violent hurricanes.

NEPTUNE

Neptune has the most violent weather in the solar system. Winds blow at over 2,000 kilometres per hour, ten times faster than hurricane winds on Earth. Methane in Neptune's atmosphere gives the planet a deep blue colour. Triton is the largest of Neptune's 14 moons that scientists know about so far. There are active volcanoes on Triton's surface.

GALAXIES

*A galaxy is a collection of dust, gases, and billions or even **trillions** of stars, all held together by gravity. Scientists used to think that our galaxy was the only one, but Edwin Hubble (see page 7) studied super-bright stars called cepheids. He worked out that they were millions of light years away, much farther away than stars in our galaxy. There must, therefore, be galaxies other than our own. Astronomers now believe that there are billions of galaxies in the universe.*

CLUSTERS

Galaxies join together in groups called clusters. Groups of clusters form superclusters. Our own galaxy, the Milky Way, is part of a cluster called the Local Group.

THE LOCAL GROUP AND AROUND 100 OTHER GALAXIES FORM A SUPERCLUSTER CALLED THE LANIAKEA SUPERCLUSTER.

The Triangulum Galaxy is part of the Local Group, which is made up of around 30 galaxies.

Gravity sometimes pulls galaxies together so that they collide. Whole clusters of galaxies can collide. These collisions take millions of years to happen. The Milky Way and Andromeda, the largest galaxy in our cluster, are on a collision course and will eventually crash into one another. But don't worry – it will be about four billion years from now!

Astronomers describe galaxies according to their shape. There are three main types.

ELLIPTICALS

These galaxies are often oval-shaped, like a rugby ball or an egg. The largest elliptical galaxies are over a million light years in **diameter**. They are the largest type of galaxy in the universe. Ellipticals mostly contain very old stars. Very few new stars form in elliptical galaxies because they don't contain the dust and gases needed for stars to be born.

SPIRALS

Spiral galaxies have a central hub of stars. Spiral arms curve outwards from the hub. Some spirals, called barred-spiral galaxies, have a bar of stars, dust and gases across them, which astronomers think are the birth places of new stars. Our own galaxy, the Milky Way, is a barred-spiral galaxy.

Spiral galaxies look like giant pinwheels.

IRREGULARS

Irregular galaxies have no fixed shape. Scientists think this may be because they were formed by two galaxies crashing into one another. Irregulars contain lots of young stars.

The Small Magellanic Cloud is a small irregular galaxy near the Milky Way.

STARS

Stars are gigantic, dazzling balls of burning gases, mostly hydrogen and helium. The pulling force of gravity squashes these gases into a ball. At the centre of the ball, the temperature becomes so hot that a process called **nuclear fusion** takes place. This releases energy as light and heat.

STARS APPEAR TO TWINKLE BECAUSE, WHEN LIGHT PASSES THROUGH THE EARTH'S ATMOSPHERE, IT IS AFFECTED BY WIND AND TEMPERATURE CHANGES. THIS BENDS THE LIGHT IN ALL DIRECTIONS, CAUSING THE TWINKLING THAT WE SEE FROM EARTH.

This is the constellation Orion. It is named after a hunter from Greek mythology.

Orion's Club

Orion's Head

Orion's Shield

Betelgeuse

Orion's Belt

Horsehead Nebula

Orion Nebula

CONSTELLATIONS

Since ancient times, man has tried to see patterns in the stars and has named these patterns after mythological creatures and heroes. Patterns of stars are called constellations. The ancient Greeks knew of 48 constellations, but modern astronomers use a total of 88 constellations to work out the position of objects in the sky. The stars in a constellation may look close together but, in fact, they could be hundreds of light years apart.

Stars are born in nebulae (the name for more than one nebula). Nebulae are clouds of gases and dust in space.

DWARFS AND GIANTS

When we look at stars, they all seem to be white dots. If we use a telescope to look, however, they are actually different colours and sizes. The colour depends on how hot the surface of the star is. Red stars are cool, only around 3,500°C. Yellow stars, like our Sun, are medium hot. Blue stars are the hottest.

Their surface temperature can reach 45,000°C. The smallest stars are called red dwarfs. Orange, yellow, yellow-white, and blue-white stars follow in order of size. The biggest of all are called blue supergiants and blue hypergiants.

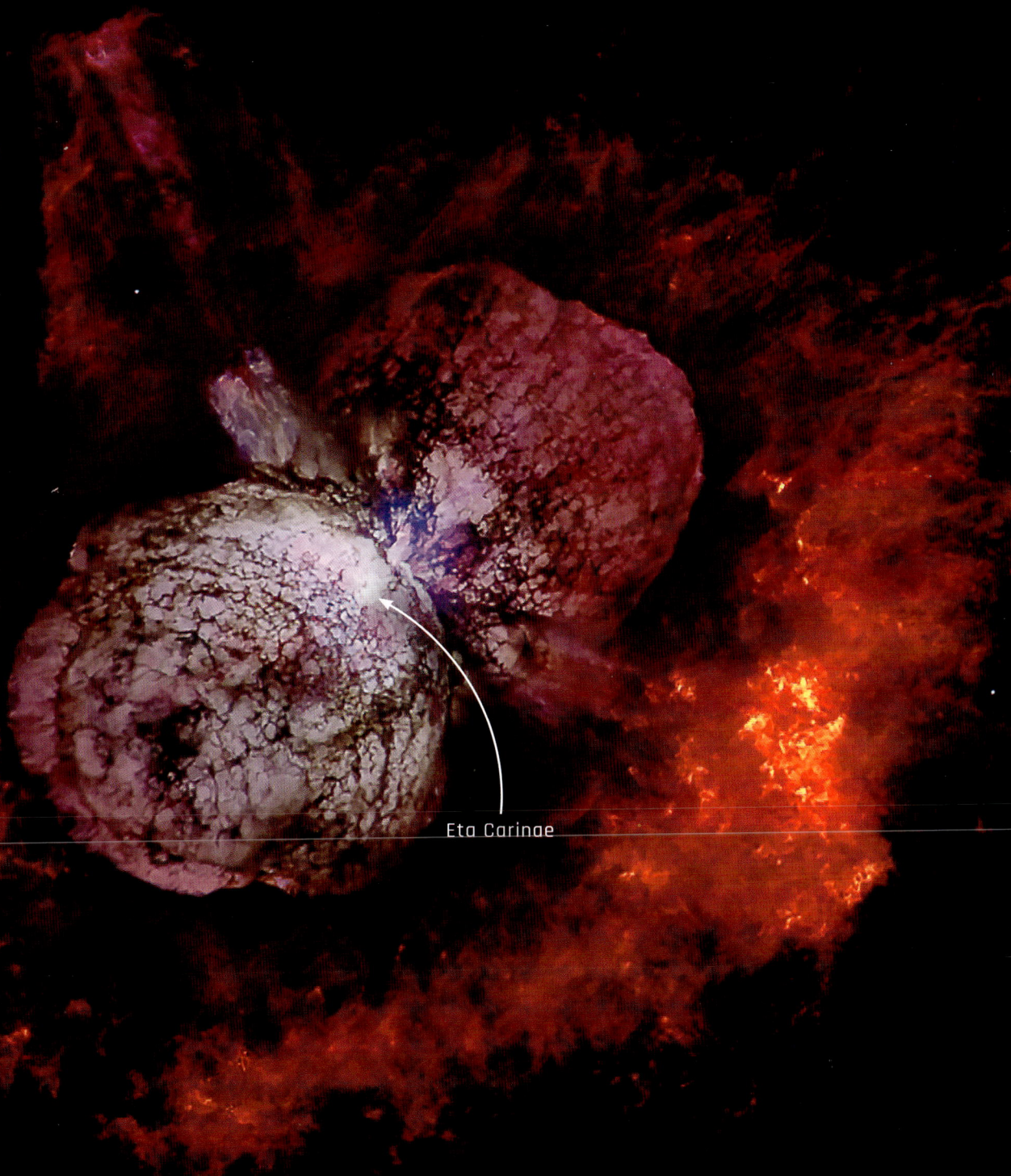

Eta Carinae

Eta Carinae is a blue hypergiant star in our galaxy. It is about five million times brighter than the Sun and its **mass** is over 100 times greater.

15

LIFE CYCLE OF A STAR

When the temperature at the core of a new star reaches around 15 million°C, nuclear fusion starts and the star begins to shine brightly. At this stage, it is called a main sequence star.

Brightly shining new-born stars light up the nebula in which they are formed.

The hot gases inside the star push back against the force of gravity, which is trying to make the star collapse in on itself. When the star runs out of hydrogen fuel in its core, it can no longer stand up to the pull of gravity and it begins to die.

LIFE SPAN OF A STAR

The life span of a star – how long it lives – and the way in which it dies depends on its size. Massive stars shine very brightly, but they have a short life-span because they use their fuel quickly. When the fuel is used up, the star swells into a red supergiant. Small stars have less fuel but, because they use it slowly, they shine for hundreds of billions of years before fading away. Find out what happens to medium-mass stars like our Sun on page 29.

Big stars eventually die in a dramatic explosion called a **supernova**. The outer layers of the star smash into the core then zoom back into space at speeds up to 10,000 kilometres per second. Betelgeuse is expected to die in a supernova explosion within the next 100,000 years.

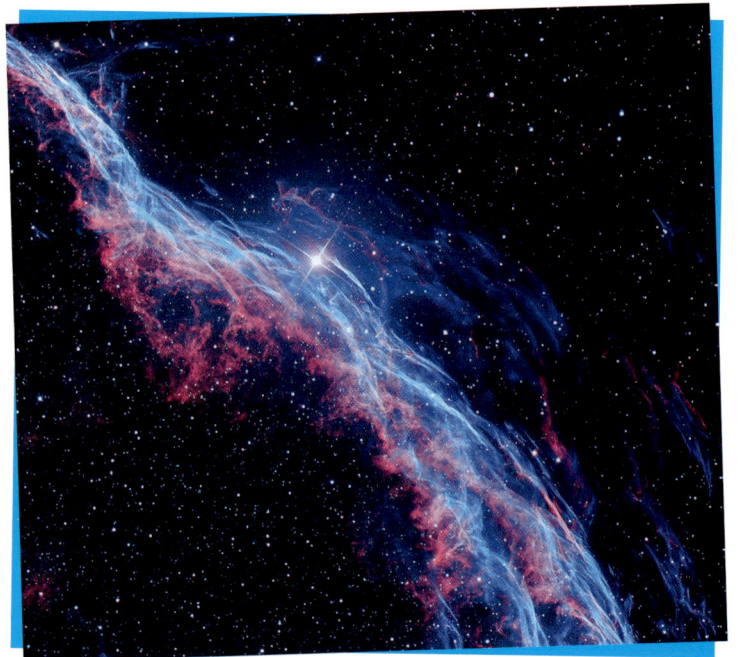

The dust and gases in the Witch's Broom Nebula are the remains of a supernova.

RECYCLING

'Stellar evolution' is the term used to describe the different stages that a star goes through during its life. Every galaxy holds stars which are at different stages of their lives, from new-born to dying. Galaxies are like massive recycling centres. Matter from supernova explosions or from red giant stars – which gradually lose their outer layers as they die – forms new nebulae. In turn, these become the birth place of new stars.

Supernova Explosion

Red Giant Star

WHITE AND BLACK DWARFS

OUR SUN WILL EVENTUALLY BECOME A WHITE DWARF.

After the outer layers of a red giant have been cast off into space, the core left behind is crushed down into a small, brilliant star called a white dwarf. Billions of years later, white dwarfs will have given off all their remaining heat and will have become cold, dead stars called black dwarfs.

DIAMONDS IN THE SKY

Many white dwarf stars have a core made of **carbon**. Over millions of years, as these white dwarfs slowly cool down, the carbon is changed into a different form – diamonds. So there really are diamonds in the sky!

DWARF PLANETS, ASTEROIDS
AND COMETS

Charon

DWARF PLANETS

Dwarf planets orbit the Sun just like other planets, but they are much smaller. There are five recognised dwarf planets in the solar system: Ceres, Pluto, Haumea, Makemake and Eris. Scientists think many more will be discovered. Pluto was once classed as a planet, but in 2006 it was re-named a dwarf planet.

Pluto

Like the Earth, Pluto has its own moon, called Charon.

ASTEROIDS

Asteroids are lumps of rock that follow their own orbit around the Sun. They are mostly found in the Asteroid Belt between Mars and Jupiter. Asteroids are made up of the material left over when the four rocky inner planets formed. There are millions of them whizzing around in space and they range in size from hundreds of miles wide to the size of a small pebble. Asteroids are also known as minor planets. Occasionally, asteroids collide with one another or they may crash into moons or planets.

Asteroids that hit the Earth's surface are called meteorites.

This huge crater in Coconino, Arizona, USA was caused by a 40-metre-wide meteorite that crashed into the Earth 50,000 years ago.

COMETS

Like asteroids, comets are made up of material left over when the planets formed, billions of years ago. Comets are made up of ice and dust particles. They orbit the Sun, usually in an oval shape.

Halley's Comet is visible from Earth every 75 years. It was last seen in 1986, before returning to deep space.

When a comet's orbit takes it close to the Sun, the ice is warmed by the Sun and the comet gives off a 'tail' of dust and gas. Some scientists think that, billions of years ago, comets collided with the Earth and that the ice they contained was the source of the water on our planet.

The Hale-Bopp comet could be seen clearly from the Earth in 1997. The blue tail is made of gases. The white tail is made of dust particles.

THE ROSETTA MISSION

In 2004, a European spacecraft called Rosetta was launched on a mission to a comet called Comet 67P. It took ten years to get there! Over the next two years, the Rosetta mission provided scientists with images and information that helped them to understand more about comets. They found, for example, that the remains of mini-comets join together to form large comets. They called these mini comets 'goosebumps'!

The Rosetta Spacecraft

EXPLORING SPACE

In 1543, even before telescopes were invented, the Polish astronomer Nicolaus Copernicus worked out that the Earth and other planets orbited the Sun.

In the 17th century, the British scientist Isaac Newton was the first person to understand that it is the pulling force of gravity that keeps the Moon in orbit around the Earth and the planets in orbit around the Sun.

Statue of Copernicus With His Model of the Universe

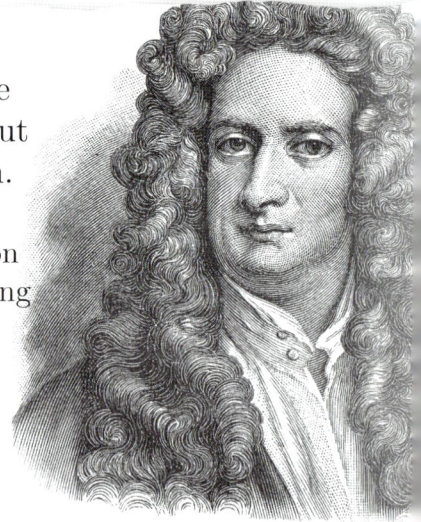

Isaac Newton

TELESCOPES

Early astronomers used telescopes to study fuzzy shapes containing pinpoints of bright light that we now know are galaxies. Modern telescopes can be launched into orbit around the Earth. The James Webb Telescope will provide even more information than The Hubble Telescope (see page 7). Using a giant mirror almost seven metres across, it will collect light from the most distant parts of space.

THE APOLLO MOON MISSIONS

In the 1960s and early 1970s, **NASA** flew **astronauts** to the Moon on board the Apollo space rockets. On the 20th of July, 1969, Neil Armstrong became the first man to walk on the Moon. Television pictures showed that the surface of the Moon is covered by rocks and craters. Although space travel is difficult and expensive, we hope to send people to Mars in the future.

NEIL ARMSTRONG'S MOON WALK WAS WATCHED LIVE ON TELEVISION BY 500 MILLION PEOPLE AROUND THE WORLD.

Astronauts landed on the Moon using a special landing craft called a Lunar Module (LM). Six manned landings were made between 1969 and 1972.

Space stations are laboratories for studying space. They have been in orbit around the Earth since the early 1970s. When they are needed, supplies, equipment and astronauts are sent up to the space station aboard rockets.

A Space Shuttle Launch

EXPLORING OTHER PANETS

Scientists have sent many unmanned spacecraft to land on the surface of other planets, including Venus, Mars, and one of Saturn's moons, Titan. Special spacecraft sent to Mars, called Mars Exploration Rovers, or MERs, have been some of the most successful. The rovers carry lasers to break up rocks and high definition cameras to send clear images back to Earth.

Some spacecraft study planets without landing. A NASA spacecraft called New Horizons was launched in 2006. In July 2015, it passed the dwarf planet Pluto and sent back pictures of Pluto's moons. One of the moons, called Nix, wobbles as it orbits Pluto! An unmanned spacecraft called Galileo spent eight years from 1995 to 2003 orbiting Jupiter. It discovered salty oceans underneath the ice on the surface of Jupiter's moon, Europa. Galileo was launched from the space shuttle Atlantis in 1989.

After launching its spacecraft into space, a space shuttle comes in to land.

BLACK HOLES

Black holes are some of the most exciting and scary things in the universe. They are objects in space that have such a strong gravitational pull that nothing can escape from them, not even light. There are two types of black hole: stellar and supermassive.

STELLAR BLACK HOLES

Most black holes form when a very large star runs out of fuel and dies in a supernova. The core of the dead star cannot stand up to the force of its own gravity, and collapses in on itself, pulling everything inwards. Within a tiny fraction of a second, it shrinks to a single point, smaller even than an atom. An enormous amount of matter is now crammed into this tiny point. The greater the mass of any object, the stronger the force of gravity it exerts. Anything that gets too close to a black hole is sucked in by this gravity, never to be seen again!

Stellar Black Hole

Singularity:
The mass of a black hole is contained in a single point called a singularity.

Event Horizon:
Anything that crosses the event horizon will be sucked into the black hole.

Accretion Disc:
Dust particles, gases and matter from dead stars swirl around black holes in a disc shape.

SUPERMASSIVE BLACK HOLES

Supermassive black holes are much bigger than stellar black holes. They are often millions or even billions of times the size of the Sun. Supermassive black holes are found at the centres of galaxies. The whirling clouds of super-hot gases and dust around supermassive black holes are the brightest objects in the universe.

Sagittarius A is the supermassive black hole at the centre of the Milky Way. Its mass is around four million times that of the Sun.

SPAGHETTIFICATION

Spaghettification is the stretching of objects into long thin shapes – just like spaghetti. Spaghettification happens when objects cross the event horizon and are drawn into a black hole. The pulling force of gravity that the black hole exerts is stronger on the side of the object closer to the black hole than on the opposite side of the object. This stretches the object, just like pulling on an elastic band. Nothing can survive this force of gravity.

IN A GALAXY CLUSTER CALLED PERSEUS, THERE IS A BLACK HOLE WHICH GIVES OUT AN EERIE NOISE. THE NOTE IS A B FLAT AND IS PITCHED 57 OCTAVES LOWER THAN MIDDLE C. IT IS THE LOWEST-PITCHED SOUND IN THE ENTIRE UNIVERSE.

Spaghettification stretches and then rips apart objects that are sucked into a black hole.

DARK ENERGY AND
DARK MATTER

Scientists have answered many questions about space, but there are still some tricky problems to solve. Two of these are dark energy and dark matter. We cannot see them, but we know they're out there!

DARK ENERGY

In the 1990s, astronomers began to measure how fast the Universe had been expanding since the Big Bang. They thought that the fast expansion that happened straight after the Big Bang would have slowed down, once stars and galaxies formed. Instead, they found, to their amazement, that not only is the Universe getting bigger, but that the rate at which it is getting bigger is also speeding up. This is called the 'accelerating universe' and is caused by dark energy.

Edwin Hubble

DARK ENERGY AND GRAVITY

All objects that have mass exert the pulling force of gravity on objects around them – the bigger the mass, the greater the gravity. Gravity should be pulling galaxies together, but the distance between them is getting bigger. Some mysterious force must be overcoming the pulling force of gravity. Dark energy is the name given to this mysterious force.

DARK MATTER

Matter is the 'stuff' that makes up everything we can touch or see, from an ant to the Moon. Astronomers call this 'ordinary matter'. Astronomers have realised that the amount of ordinary matter in space is only a very small part of all the matter that they know is out there. They know this because the amount of ordinary matter is nowhere near enough to explain the amount of gravity in the universe. As we have seen, dark energy makes up most of the gap, but the rest is called dark matter. Dark matter does not give off any light and cannot be seen, even using powerful telescopes. The only way we know it is there is because it too exerts its own gravity.

THE MILKY WAY HAS A HALO – OR CIRCLE OF LIGHT – MADE UP OF GROUPS OF OLD STARS. MORE THAN HALF OF THE MASS OF THE MILKY WAY IS IN THIS HALO, BUT MOST OF IT IS INVISIBLE DARK MATTER.

WHAT IS DARK MATTER MADE OF?

Scientists don't really know what dark matter is. One idea is WIMPs! This stands for Weakly Interacting Massive Particles – particles that are present everywhere, which can pass through ordinary matter, without causing any effect. If billions of these particles exist, they might together make up all the missing matter.

What Is The Universe Made Of?

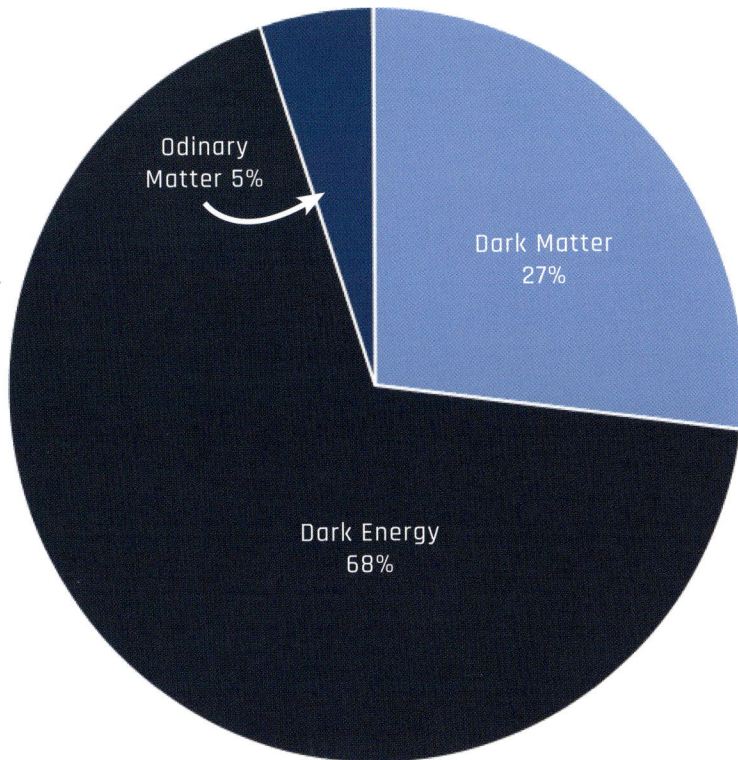

Odinary Matter 5%

Dark Matter 27%

Dark Energy 68%

QUASARS ARE SOME OF THE BRIGHTEST OBJECTS IN THE UNIVERSE, SHINING SO BRIGHTLY THAT THEY OUTSHINE ALL OTHER STARS IN THEIR GALAXY. A HUGE CLUSTER OF 73 QUASARS, CALLED THE HUGE LARGE QUASAR GROUP, HAS BEEN DISCOVERED NINE BILLION LIGHT YEARS AWAY FROM THE EARTH.

Omega Centauri is a group of old stars, called a globular cluster, in the halo of our galaxy.

IS ANYONE OUT THERE ?

Scientists have always looked for signs of life elsewhere in the universe. Nothing has been found so far, but space is so vast that it seems unlikely that Earth is the only planet where life is found. What do you think?

LIFE ON MARS?

Scientists think that, long ago, Mars was warmer and wetter and that, therefore, life might once have existed there. It is thought that future discoveries on Mars by rover craft might include buried fossils. In 1996, scientists thought that they had found fossilised bacteria in a meteorite from Mars, found in Antarctica. Other scientists disagreed.

Photographs of Mars suggest that water once flowed on the surface. This water may have allowed life to exist.

IN APRIL 2017, NASA'S CASSINI SPACECRAFT PICKED UP THE FIRST CLUES THAT THERE COULD BE **MICROBES** ON ONE OF SATURN'S MOONS, ENCELADUS. THESE MICROBES COULD BE LIVING IN THE WARM SEAS, DEEP BELOW THE ICE THAT COVERS THE SURFACE.

LITTLE GREEN MEN

In 1967, an astronomer named Jocelyn Bell working in Cambridge in the UK managed to detect radio signals from space. She named them LGM – short for Little Green Men. In fact, instead of aliens from other planets, Bell had discovered the first pulsar star. Pulsars are dead stars that spin quickly and give out pulses of energy.

The Allen Telescope Array is a group of 42 radio telescopes that try to pick up radio signals from deep space. Such signals could suggest life exists elsewhere in the universe.

EXOPLANETS

Exoplanets are planets outside our solar system, which are orbiting a star. Since the first exoplanet was found in 1995, over a thousand more have been discovered. Some of these are so similar to the Earth that scientists think life may exist on them, even though no sign of life has been discovered so far.

Exoplanet Orbiting its Red Giant Star

Red giants form when the cores of old stars heat up, causing the star to swell up.

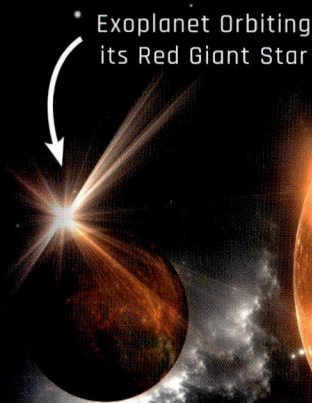

GOLDILOCKS PLANETS

No living thing on Earth can survive without water. When astronomers are looking for life elsewhere, they hunt for exoplanets that are the right temperature for liquid water to exist. These planets, called Goldilocks planets, need to be at the right distance from their star. They are neither too hot nor too cold, but just right, like Goldilocks' porridge. If they are too close, the heat from the star will **evaporate** any water and if they are too far away, any water will be frozen.

Kepler-186f is an Earth-like planet in the Milky Way galaxy that is in the 'Goldilocks zone', just the right distance from its star for life to exist.

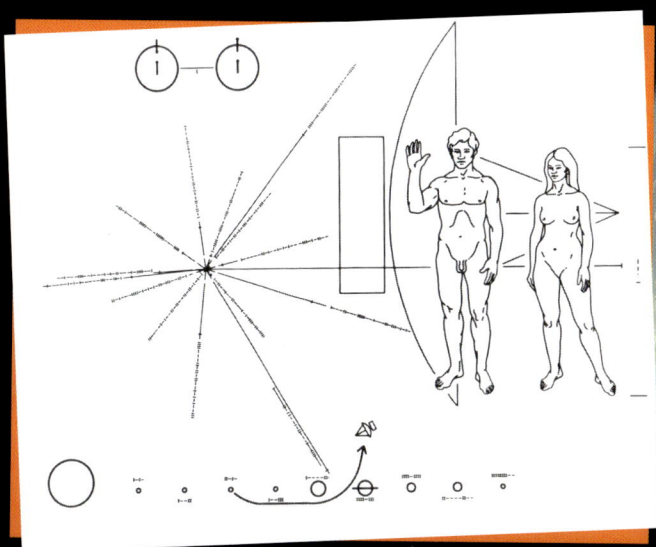

A pair of plaques was placed on board the Pioneer spacecraft in 1970s, as a way of communicating with alien life. The plaques have engraved pictures of humans and a map of the solar system. No reply has yet been received!

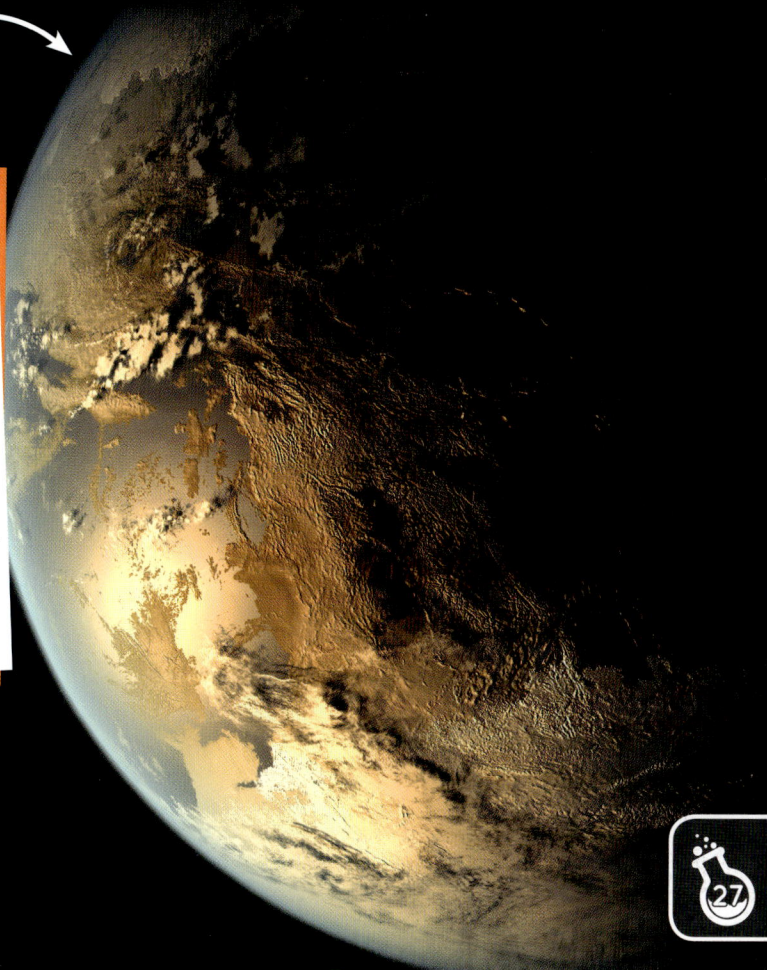

THE END OF THE UNIVERSE

Nobody really knows how, or even if, the universe will end. But don't worry – nothing will happen for billions of years. Scientists have come up with several theories about the possible end of the universe.

THE BIG CRUNCH

The universe is constantly growing, but scientists think that this can't happen forever. A point might be reached where the force of gravity causes all the matter in the universe to collapse in on itself. All matter might return to the single point from which it started. The Big Crunch would be like the Big Bang in reverse! Another Big Bang might then happen, creating a new universe, followed trillions of years later by another Big Crunch and so on. The universe that we live in now might only exist between just one Bang and one Crunch! This idea is called the Big Bounce theory.

THE BIG FREEZE

The Big Freeze or Big Chill theory suggests that the universe will keep expanding forever. If this happens, the distance between galaxies will grow, old stars will burn themselves out and no new stars will form. The universe will gradually cool to become dead, empty and extremely cold. No life could survive in these conditions.

THE BIG RIP

Astronomers think that the universe is growing at a faster and faster rate and that this is due to the mysterious force called dark energy (see page 24). The Big Rip theory is the opposite of the Big Crunch theory. It suggests that the force of expansion will eventually 'beat' the force of gravity. The universe will expand so fast and so violently that all matter, from atoms to entire galaxies, will be ripped apart.

DEATH OF THE SUN

The Sun gives off light because nuclear fusion takes place deep inside it. Eventually, in around five billion years, the core of the Sun will start to run out of fuel and it will swell outwards. It will turn into a red giant, many times larger than its current size. Mercury and Venus will be swallowed up. The Earth itself will melt, the oceans will boil and all water will evaporate. When all the fuel is used up, a red giant loses its outer layers. These form a glowing cloud called a planetary nebula.

IT TAKES 8.3 MINUTES FOR LIGHT TO TRAVEL TO EARTH FROM THE SUN. THE SUN THEREFORE DOESN'T LOOK AS IT IS NOW, BUT AS IT LOOKED 8.3 MINUTES AGO!

This planetary nebula, called the Helix Nebula, is also known as The Eye of God.

THE INTERNATIONAL SPACE STATION (ISS)

The International Space Station is a man-made satellite that continually orbits the Earth. It travels at a top speed of 27,600 kilometres per hour. Every 92 minutes, it completes an orbit of the Earth. A team of six astronauts live and work on board.

The International Space Station

WHY IS THE ISS IMPORTANT?

The ISS enables scientists to find out what happens to people when they live in space. Most astronauts stay on board for about six months. Scientists have also learned how to keep a spacecraft working over a long period of time. NASA plans to one day send humans deeper into space than ever before and the ISS is one of the first steps towards making this happen.

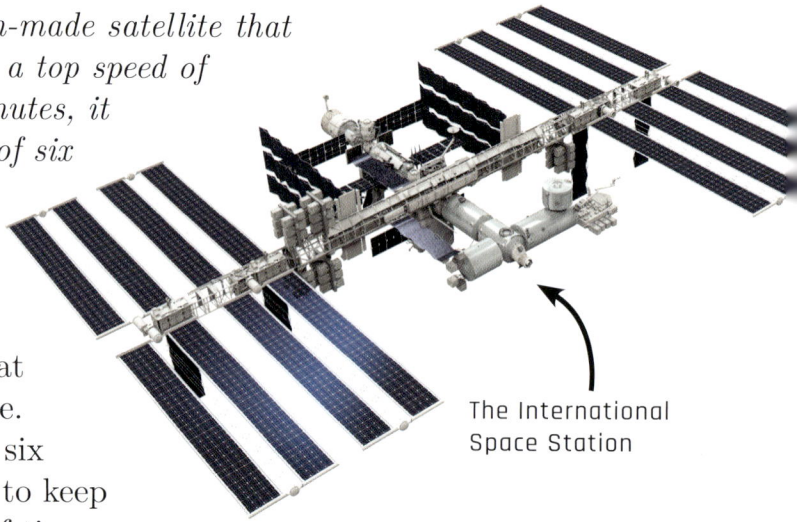

ON BOARD

The ISS is as big as a large house, with five bedrooms, two bathrooms and a gymnasium. Astronauts have to exercise for two hours a day to keep their muscles strong. New crew members enter through special doors called docking ports. On the outside are robot arms that helped to build the ISS and now help to move astronauts around outside when they are carrying out experiments.

Strong tethers keep the astronauts firmly attached to the ISS when they are working outside.

MANY COUNTRIES INCLUDING THE USA, RUSSIA, JAPAN, CANADA AND EUROPEAN COUNTRIES WORKED TOGETHER TO BUILD THE ISS.

GLOSSARY

asteroids	small, rocky bodies orbiting the Sun
astronauts	people who are trained to travel and work in a spacecraft
atmosphere	the layer of gases surrounding the Earth or another planet
atoms	the smallest possible units of a chemical element, such as hydrogen
axis	the imaginary line that passes through the centre of a star or planet and around which the star or planet spins
billion	a thousand million
carbon	a non-metallic element that occurs naturally in different forms including charcoal and diamond
carbon dioxide	a colourless gas naturally found in the atmosphere of some planets
celestial bodies	objects that occur naturally in outer space
comets	small icy bodies found in the remotest parts of the solar system
debris	scattered pieces of rubbish
diameter	the distance through the centre of an object
evaporate	turn from a liquid into a vapour
gravity	the force that pulls all objects that have mass towards one another
helium	a gas found inside stars that is the second most common element in the universe
hydrogen	a colourless gas that is by far the most common element in the universe
mass	the amount of matter that something contains
matter	the physical substance – or stuff – that things are made of
methane	a colourless gas that is easily set on fire
microbes	a life form that can only be seen with a microscope
million	a thousand thousand
moons	any natural bodies in space that are orbiting a planet
NASA	the National Aeronautics and Space Administration – an organisation in the USA that is responsible for space science
nuclear fusion	a process in which the nuclei (centres) of atoms join or fuse together and release large amounts of energy
orbit	to move around another body in space, held in place by its gravity
particles	extremely small pieces of a solid, liquid or gas
radiation	energy given off in the form of heat or light
satellites	man-made objects that orbit planets or moons to collect information or for communication purposes
solar system	the Sun and all the planets, comets and asteroids that orbit around it
space shuttle	a reusable spacecraft, launched from a rocket
supernova	the explosion of a massive star at the end of its life
telescope	a piece of equipment, used to study space, designed to make something appear closer than it actually is
theory	an idea put forward to explain something
trillions	a million million

INDEX